T0154403

BAD JUDGMENT

POEMS

Cathleen Calbert

Sarabande  *Books*

LOUISVILLE, KENTUCKY

FIRST EDITION

Managing Editor
Sarabande Books, Inc.
2234 Dundee Road, Suite 200
Louisville, KY 40205

LIBRARY OF CONGRESS CATALOGING-IN-PUBLICATION DATA

Calbert, Cathleen.
    Bad judgment : poems / by Cathleen Calbert. — 1st ed.
        p.   cm.
    ISBN 1-889330-23-X (cloth : alk. paper). — ISBN 1-889330-24-8 (pbk. : alk. paper)
    I. Title.
    PS3553.A39448B3   1999
    811'.54—dc21   98-19571
                                                                     CIP

Cover Painting: Titian (Tiziano Vecellio). *Venus of Urbino.* Uffizi, Florence, Italy.
Used by kind permission, Scala/Art Resource, NY.

Cover and text design by Charles Casey Martin.

Manufactured in the United States of America.
This book is printed on acid-free paper.

Sarabande Books is a nonprofit literary organization.

for Christopher Mayo
and
in memory of Lynda Schraufnagel

ACKNOWLEDGMENTS

Grateful acknowledgment is made to the editors of the following publications, in which these poems first appeared, sometimes in different versions:

Feminist Studies: "Dream Babies"
Harvard Review: "The Woman Who Loved Things"
Literature and Psychology: "When the World Lost Meaning"
Nedge: "Providence"
The New Republic: "When Nights Were Full of Sex and Churches"
Nimrod: "When Forever Began"
The Ohio Review: "After the Tragedy," "The Last Angel Poem," "Dear
    Lynda," (under the title "Lynda"), "The Vampire Cat"
The Paris Review: "In Praise of My Young Husband"
Poetry East: "Lunatic Snow"
Poetry Northwest: "Bad Judgment," "Dead Debutante," "A Lady with a
    Pomeranian," "My Dead Boyfriend," "My Summer as a
    Bride," "The Vampire Baby"
TriQuarterly: "Trinity"
Western Humanities Review: "Dark Water," "Floating"
Zone 3: "Beyond the Power of Positive Thinking"

"Lunatic Snow" was reprinted in *Literature and Psychology* and "The Woman Who Loved Things" in *The Best American Poetry 1995.*

"Dark Water," "Deer," "In Praise of My Young Husband," "My Summer as a Bride," "Providence," and "When Forever Began" appeared in a limited edition chapbook, *My Summer as a Bride*, published by Riverstone Press in 1995.

I also would like to thank the Corporation of Yaddo, the MacDowell Colony, and Rhode Island College for their generous support.

TABLE OF CONTENTS

When Nights Were Full of Sex and Churches

Three chimes, and it's everyone I've ever slept with,
even once, even just barely, swept free into the light
of a cloudless moon, waving, *hi, hi.* They are drunk, pale,
silly upside down, their shoes dancing above their heads.
These many men are smiling, looking down, seeing me.
I can hear the happy clatter of their dangling genitals.
But why can't I see a cow with pretty eyes, a gold chicken
in a peasant sky? Why can't I be that red-haired woman
sleeping in Chagall's heavenly tree? Then I could dream
of wedding veils, floating higher, turning blue
in a world made of colors and marital sex, happiness,
breasts painted into big circles, childlike hands at ease.
In my night sky, I have only men, harmonizing:
There was a serpent who loved to sing, there was,
there was, hiss hiss. Thus, he forsook his serpenting
because he was in love, he was. Finished, they blow kisses
through transparent lips as though they have given me
something at last, but at the sound of midnight horns,
they leave as spooks do: easily. I open a real window,
calling after them: *I remember. I still have a red dress*
hanging behind the sheaves of blue gauze in my closet.

Trinity

Woman as wild card, as other
than wife, mother, lover, friend,
than the ones you've fucked or never wanted to fuck,

I am the single woman as dinner guest,
wondrous, lovely anomaly, odd woman out,
sole, solo, solitaire, night's queen,

unescorted, unchaperoned, unaccompanied
(unhusbanded, unasked, unwooed), vestal, heart-whole,
gendered, gentle woman, just a joker

in the living room, on the balcony, by the begonias,
drinking couples' wine, scotch, vodka, strawberry tea,
eating couples' clams, linguine, lobster, lettuce leaves,

friendly to the wives, liking the wives
(having been a wife, wanting to be a wife again),
wanting the wives to like me because I like them

(and because I want to be invited back again),
too friendly to the men, liking the men
(having had a man, wanting to have a man again

before I die and am placed alone, cold, in that last
deep bed of this shared green world; that is,
wanting to get off, get even, get lucky, get laid)

though I remain unnameable, unapproachable, untouchable,
the best you could have, boys, but not quite worth it,
after all, my friends, not quite worth it at all in the end.

So for a short space, let me stand for "space." Let me be
the space in your lives. A portal, an opening, a break.
Call me "O." Fill in the gap. Pencil me in: the big zero.

Then flatten this figure into three planes (use your right
hands, please, for the left sting with wedding rings),
and, oh, for a space, let us triangulate:

all you wives chopping, frying, mincing, sighing, talking,
laughing, lacking that essential mystery, and omitted,
I'm sad to say, momentarily, discarded as you are

by all you men patting my knee, back, arm, face,
offering things to eat, drink, smoke, try, taste,
applauding my hair, socks, dog, blouse, name,

asking: do I like to ski, cook, read, rent movies?
Would I go for a walk, a swim, a ride, for coffee?
To see the countryside, local color, compost heap?

Privately expressing concern, interest, curiosity:
my job, my dog, my cacti, cough, calligraphy.
What do I lack, desire, do without, need?

Telling me (confidentially) how you would love
to come to town, come visit, come see me
if only you could find time, make space, get free.

Yes, my dears, had we but world enough,
and time and again I leave as I came, sexy to men
because I'm not sleeping with any of them,

going home alone while all the husbands sleep
with all the wives, wives with their husbands,
the whole world falling to a lazy, angry sleep,

"unfulfilled," fucked up, fantasizing,
in each other's arms, legs, plans, schemes,
as the stars get it up to shine once again

for you and for me (forgive our trespasses),
and the crickets count out a beat to our lives,
and I kiss my dog, who sleeps at my feet.

Beyond the Power of Positive Thinking

I am letting myself have a well puppy,
my mother's blood pressure decrease,
and the engine in my car run easily.

I've stopped holding on to negative energy
and no longer need academic poverty.
I am radiant and free, calm and serene.

It's okay to have a green Mercedes.
I can accept a green Mercedes.
A green Mercedes is okay with me.

We are living in a land of plenty.
There's enough for everybody
if we all rechannel our energy,

so I'm setting free the seven hearts
within to ensure my rapture and give
me enough divinity for everything.

It's up to us. If we can just keep clear,
keep clean, keep concentrating, we will
never even need to stop breathing.

The Woman Who Loved Things

A woman finally learned to love things, so things learned
to love her too as she pressed herself to their shining sides,
their porous surfaces. She smoothed along walls until walls
smoothed along her as well, a joy, a climax, this flesh
against plaster, the sweet suck of consenting molecules.

Sensitive men and women became followers, wrapping
themselves in violet, pasting her image over their hearts,
pressing against walls until walls came to appreciate
differences in molecules. This became a worship.
They became a love. A church. A cult. A way of being.

Of course, it had to happen: the woman's love kept growing
until she was loved by trees and appliances, from toasters
to natural obstacles, until her ceiling shook loose to send kisses,
sheets wound themselves between her legs, and floorboards
broke free of their nails, straining their lengths over her sleeping.

She awoke and drove out of town alone. In love, rocks flew
through her windows, then whole hillsides slid, loosening
with desire. The car shattered its shaft to embrace her,
but she ran from the wreckage, calling all the sweet things
as she waited in a field of strangely complacent daisies.

She spoke of love until losing her breath, and the things
trilled to feel that loss too, sighing in thingness. She fell
down, and the things fell down around her. She cried
Christ! and the things cried *Christ!* in their thing-hearts
until everything living and unliving wonderfully collided.

My Dead Boyfriend

I hoped no one would notice anything
    as we toured gay *Paris,*
        but I had no need to worry.
My companions didn't know him well,
    couldn't compare this to that:
        the frigid skin, stiff expression,
his arm frozen around my waist.
    People notice less than you think.
        I was grateful for the temporary
reanimation of my sweetheart, a final holiday,
    though his face stayed gray, unhealthy looking,
        and he didn't especially feel up
to visiting any famous French cemeteries.
    He preferred clubbing, blowing smoke rings,
        ordering drinks, and dancing slowly.
When we made love, he was hard as a rock
    but couldn't come, so he satisfied me
        and left me feeling a little empty.
The last time he climbed on my body,
    I felt a shudder, then the cool semen
        finally pumping before he seized up
permanently. On his way to the grave,
    he'd wanted to give me something: a baby.
        I appreciated these inhuman exertions
and stroked the cold, clenched hands
    as he relaxed into the corpse he needed to be.
        I could feel his seed inside,
like tears of ice melting.
    But what had he given me?
        When your man is dead,

can he create something new and living?
    No, I would bear a half-dead baby,
        whose cheeks stayed rosy
though his eyes iced blue, lips rigid
    at my swollen, hungry breasts
        as I sang him songs
of the spider and the rain and the sun,
    then tucked him in the icebox
        to keep him cozy while I cried
myself to sleep, thinking somewhere
    mothers are strolling in the park,
        not dreaming in the dark mid-morning,
somewhere men don't need to be
    resurrected daily, babies laugh and breathe,
        and women aren't the only ones living.

Bad Judgment

It's on the line,
    the sun's in your eyes,
        the time you thought it would be all right
            to go for a drive alone at night,
                he didn't mean it,
                he'll never do it again,
        you can trust him,
    I think she's really a friend,
I bet the child will be all right where he is,
    it doesn't get dark until late,
        I'll take the red-eye,
            have the cheese steak,
                you keep track of the receipts,
            we'll only meet for coffee,
    I'll weigh less in a couple weeks,
    I'll take the job,
I'll marry him,
    I'll see my mother in the spring,
        no hurry,
            I'm not even sleepy,
                I can drive all night, don't worry,
            shall we get some cigarettes?
    How about chocolate martinis?
Is the water supposed to be green?
It's all right, I'm not ovulating,
    it's all right, I'm clean,
        it's all right, I haven't been with anyone else lately,
            having a baby will bring us closer together,
                I can stand another cup of coffee,
        let's get the puppy,

let's get the aquarium,
let's get another puppy,
I think that's as big as a dog like that gets,
he's just lonely,
why don't we not plan anything?
If the book's good, they'll publish it eventually,
why don't we paint the whole thing?
We could knock down a wall,
we could dig up these trees,
I think I'll wait to have a baby,
I bet these sores don't mean anything,
my doctor knows what's best for me,
my dentist knows what's best for me,
my therapist knows I'm trying,
I feel I'll never lose you, we'll keep writing,
you're sensitive, that's why you do these things,
I'll just watch a little TV,
I'll talk to him, but I won't say anything,
we'll talk, but we won't do anything,
if I tell him how I feel,
if he tells me how he feels,
I want him to be honest with me,
I only want to know the truth,
not knowing hurts worse,
henna just makes your hair shiny,
it's too overcast to burn,
he's staying for the children,
she doesn't understand him,
they're not even sleeping together,
everybody parks here,

they never ticket,

they almost never tow,

there's an undertow

but you hardly feel it,

this will pinch a little,

this might smart,

you'll only feel a tug,

are you crazy, they love company!

I don't think she meant anything,

why don't you go talk to her?

I bet the two of you can straighten it out,

if I were you, I'd leave him,

I'd perm my hair,

I'd get that outfit,

I only want what's best for you,

I know you do,

I love you too.

When Forever Began

He's leaning into me, whispering, *darling,*
I love you madly, and I'm thinking, *why mad?*
Wanting to be loved sanely for a change,
wishing I could stop writing fragments to friends
in a strange, rhythmic scrawl: *I'm crazy about him.*
We're mad for each other. Can you get me out of here?
I'm righting the glasses he's romantically knocked aside,
then blindly crossing the dark bar, fumbling my way
into the women's room, where I find "Fran & Joey
4-ever 3/18 1:00 a.m." Is this when forever began?
Wiping my hands, I turn around to see "Paul & Amy
6 months & more." *Than what?* I ask. I'm stumbling

back to him, and he's leaning into me, gently
burning my ear on his cigarette. Brushing ashes
down my blouse, he vows, *I'd never do anything*
to hurt you, but I recall my mother telling me,
I wouldn't hurt you for the whole world,
and how, though small, I would be thinking,
why would the whole world want you to?
I have never understood the language of love.
Still, he's pulling me close. *Dear,* he is saying,
shall we marry, we're mad, mad for each other.
And I, not understanding, whisper back,
If you mean what I think you mean, okay.

Dream Babies

They are palm-size, pocket-size,
as small as the chicken eggs
used in "Parenting for Teens,"

paired girls and boys playing
at having babies for a week.
I guess it's a real success

if they take them seriously
(egg raw, egg ready), a victory
when one girl collapses

into tears on the sixth day,
jelly slipping through her
pretty, frightened fingers.

Egg-size but beyond egg
are my dream babies: pink,
perfect lives, tiny diapers

wound between their finger-
little legs, and blue their eyes,
but hard to see their smiles,

their bodies so easy to lose
in the streets of my dreams,
in blanket folds, in soiled sheets.

What have I done with them?
I only have two hands, and dream
babies can be unbelievably heavy.

So why is it hard to take them
seriously? If only I were sure
they heard me, that my words

had meaning, I would force
them to see my position:
the world is too vast a place,

and they are too small to be safe.
Sometimes, if I'm lucky enough,
I find them again. Sometimes

they even revive, singing,
but always I am at their mercy:
out of nowhere, babies.

The Vampire Baby

Unhappy at my breasts,
it scooched its sullen way

up to my neck, a sliding
white sack of baby flesh.

Lips pressing into my skin,
it seemed pleased and sent me

into dreaming of flesh
into flesh, blood-bonding,

but the baby never grew,
and even ecstasy is draining:

that pale monkey head
always under my chin.

Soon it would be keeping
secrets from me selfishly:

my hidden spoons,
stolen bottles of iodine.

A mother knows, I'd coo,
but it didn't coo to me.

We needed room to breathe.
We pleaded, *Please, just go*

to school from nine to two.
It simply grinned and drooled.

Then one fiery day the baby
came to its own conclusions,

crawling sadly into the sunset,
encircled in our ruby heirlooms.

We made love until the blue
marks disappeared. Afterward,

we were strange to one another,
put on each other's clothes,

and called into the night,
Is the baby all right?

But there was no baby,
so we curved into each other

and whispered wicked things:
how desire can turn into need.

A Lady with a Pomeranian

I would like to go home.
But I have no home.
I would like to call my husband.
But I have no husband.

I would like to be distracted
by my cute though time-consuming children,
but I have no children,
and I am not distracted.

I would like to call my dog
to my side. I have a dog,
but he is very small and has
his own problems to deal with.

I would like to call my friends.
Whenever I do, they are kind
for an hour, over the phone,
yet they live far away, alone

in their own lives, existences
face-to-face, elemental, sexless,
or they're seeing married men
who adore them (*je t'adore, je t'aime*).

Besides, they're too deep for me: *Listen,*
we are a living history. How will it read?
"At this time, women lived their lives alone,
roaming the countryside, itinerant and testy."

I'd like to know I am now and will remain free
of facial tics and uncontrollable gesturing.

I would like to have boys admire me
or even see me as I stroll along the avenue.

I would like to know I won't always live alone,
or simply that someone, sometime, somewhere
will once again have sex with me.

I'd like to know I'm not currently dying of anything.

I would like to have money.
It makes life so easy.

I'd like to know how I ended up in this city.

I mean, without having to reread
Items One through Ten
on the "List Explaining All Things."

Surely there are signs revealed to me.
To wit: a bird flew in my window.

Meaning!

I found a playing card in the street:
a Queen of Hearts.

More meaning!

My brother's house in the hills
did not go up in flames
though twenty others did.

My family lives!

Though my father's dead...
but he was mean! So you see,
it could all add up to something.

I live on Benefit Street, close to Hope,
Angell, Benevolent, Mercy.
You see what I mean.

Poe's fiancée lived two doors down from me.

(Though they never married.)

(Because of his debauchery.)

(Anyway, maybe the engagement
never meant much of anything.)

I would like to read more
because it would be good for me,
professionally speaking,

to know more at parties,
if I should be invited to parties,
but I have a siren couch and cable TV,

and it's too easy,
or I'm too easy,
or life is too hard.

I'd like to pray to God to comfort me,
but there is no God.

Or if there is a God,
He or She can't intervene,
for prayers should not, cannot, spare me
when all of us can't get off scot-free.

I'd like to go to church despite these beliefs
and meet some nice men, but I never know when
and likely would not rise in time.

I'd like to know how my friends live
without meaning. I ask them,
but they don't explain effectively

and tease me for needing Divine Revelation,
an actual sign-on-the-dotted-line deal,
no vague hints or whisperings.

I would like the world suffused with meaning,
a patchwork quilt of God's responsibility,

heavenly immanence apparent
in everything, all blessed or damned,

like how it used to be teaching
nineteenth-century novels to undergrads,
everything adding up to something:
foreshadowing, symbols, plot, theme.

I'd like to get over my Spiritual Crisis.

I would like at least to finish unpacking
and figure out about these curtains
and how to make these floors look clean
(shouldn't a woman know such things?)

and find off-street parking,
so I'd stop dreaming of the dread
Denver Boot told of so convincingly
on the red violations I keep receiving.

Then maybe I'd quit wanting to go home,
to my husband, who waits for me anxiously,
in heaven, I guess, or would if there were,
but there's not, so.... Where is he?

Where am I, he must be thinking.
He always wants to take care of me!
The porch light is on, dinner awaiting.
I would call, but it's late, it's too late,

and I am left alone with this life
that somewhere along the line
with my own God-given free will—
let's deny destiny—I must have chosen.

Floating

I.

Watching the fine lines fan into maps of my face.
Changing not as Yeats dreamed the delicious
scooping of shadows but as Maud truly aged.

Looking at pictures of Sexton, her smile becoming
an exaggeration of itself before twisting
into a disappearance.

Smoking in bed when my beautiful student
finally admits to thinking
that Plath baked to death.

(Living too long in electric kitchens?
Did he think that she, like the witch
with those fat children in that story,

jumped into the oven, leaving herself
vulnerable to baby hands that could turn
on her, turn up the temperature?)

II.

Our traditions are not like those
of the men who shoot out
a splatter of brains, leaving no hope

of coming back, even partway:
women like to resurrect for a while,
to try for a slice just to see.

"Hesitation cut," these trial dates.
Curiosity. Pandora. Eve.
An old love of opening.

After years of going down,
we know how to swallow
anything, even bodies

of water, the stones in our pockets
denying the truth that women
float more easily than men do.

Dear Lynda,

I wish you were here.
You'd like this. I'd like this
better if you were with me.

You would love this room,
the windows holding roses,
two and two and two, then

one rose, one rose, one rose.
Pink chaises longues, pink pillows.
You'd tease me for the luxury.

You'd like this, you'd like that.
You would, but you don't exist.
They burned your body in the Midwest.

So the "you" here is ash, is dust.
Yes, I remember us, but death has
your slim body, your sympathy.

I believe you may have
told Death about me,
where I live, what I drink,

but you don't speak to me,
you don't answer, you don't
care if the room is blue or pink.

You turned to dust, to ash
before I could learn to speak
and ease your misery.

Yours was no easeful dying.
You didn't swallow death
as we had dreamed of doing.

Death swallowed you whole,
your slim body, your sympathy,
and where you have gone,

I suppose I too will go.
Since you have gone, why
should I be afraid to follow?

But I am afraid.
And I blame death.
I blame you.

After the Tragedy

We put away the dishes.
Someone changed the sheets.
Windows were opened, then painted blue, and painted shut.
We wrote lists and threw the lists away.
We cashed in stocks, and we took stock of our situation.
Someone made stock for soup.
We ate soup, and we ate bread.
We said, *Bread has its history.*
We said, *I can't eat anything.*
Someone put the crusts of bread aside.
We left crumbs for the birds we hoped to see.
We called our mothers and found they were gone.
We wrote an editorial.
We wrote to our elected official.
We called the police.
We behaved badly.
We cried out, *What about me?*
We asked our old friends, *What about me?*
We called to the four winds, *What about me?*
We watched ourselves weep in the mirror to see how ugly we could be.
We broke crockery, accidentally.
We lay in the sun like sick cats, full of thin birds.
We rounded our belly in our hands.
We talked about life as shifting sands.
We said, *Our sad hands are like sieves sifting sand.*
We lost the faith of our childhood.
We slipped a sliver of faith into the lining of a checked apron.
We slipped a sliver of faith into the veins at our wrist, wondering if
    it would work its way to our heart.
We sang "Sweet Bird of Youth" and "Sweet Mystery."

Some of us requested leaves.
Red leaves turned to gold.
Water turned to wine as wives turned away from husbands.
Women turned to each other.
We all turned away from the camera.
We turned our faces away.
We turned in our badges.
We shot up the ranch.
We undid our holsters.
We waited for our fathers.
We called out *Papa* as though we had just learned to speak, as though
    we hardly knew the names of things.
We appealed to reason.
We wrote lengthy apologies.
We unplugged the phone.
We turned off the answering machine.
We found there were more red birds in trees though colors had
    faded imperceptibly.
We didn't get up in the morning.
We slept through the afternoon.
We went to bed early.
We dreamed we were dreaming of peace.
We dreamed of forgetting.
We dreamed we could remember everything.
Friends disappeared.
New friends appeared.
No one explained anything.
We said, *I will never make love again,* then we made love again.
It started raining.
The rain hurt our feelings.

The rain sounded like red birds flying.
We clapped our hands to our ears.
Certain words lost meaning: *coverlet, lover, loosely.*
The fruit in our baskets turned red with ripening.
Nothing seemed to mean much of anything.
We knew we were no longer happy.
We said, *I will never be happy again.*
We said it with meaning.
And we found that we were never happy again.
And we found that we were also happy.

The Vampire Cat

He grieved for his fallen brethren
(crashed umbrellas of the night sky,
cousin Chiroptera, sheets of skin
accordioned in) as only cats can, half-
heartedly, yawning a cry to the moon,
curling infernally, circle upon circle,
everything swerving to the round
of his sickle claws as he gazed lazily
into the lunar mirror above. Prideful,
possessing little pity, he blamed bats
for being easily forgotten: filthy ways
and lack of beauty. Rats with wings.

II

Gazing past the shoulders of the living,
he turned his Egyptian profile to the ghosts
of forebears glistening within mummies
of glazed clay, ancient evil smiling all the way
from the tailless torsos to their thin ears,
delicate neck rings. He believed in monarchy,
divine right of kings, Manifest Destiny.
Posing before portraits of Nefertiti,
he showed off the kohl around his gold eyes
and imitated Akhenaton's androgyny.
Like Cleopatra, he spoke of salad days
and, like a bourgeois, the servant problem.

III.

Why bother to control his magpie thieving,
his greed and groundless jealousy?
He preferred picking fights and being petty.
He would not even try to comprehend
deferred gratification and diddled his days
drawing up selfish maxims, applying his energy
to the rhetoric of the helpless gourmand,
crying carpe diems to the cream puff,
rhyming his joy, his need, his urgency,
his stomach swelling with hard sauce
and heavy cream, his prick glistening
as he sat, paws spread, in the sun.

IV.

He swept into the laps of my visitors,
doting particularly on Protestant ministers
and celibate students of Art or Philosophy,
nipping their fingertips, sipping their dreams
of the future and equality, until they lost
themselves to the touch of that kitty,
that soothing, that fat sensuality.
He purred the easiest of easy platitudes,
always agreeing to everything: *why not,*
the lady in an ape suit, several clever
gentlemen, cat cries, sleazy sex, then ease.
But all faded, and he grew plump, pleased.

The Last Angel Poem

They are everywhere we want them to be:
on the stems of our apples, at the garden door,

in clogged chimneys, basement crawl spaces,
our boyfriends' dirty blue jeans.

Tell the worried theologians they are
not done for. (How many can dance

on the tips of our pens? All
of the angles of angels.) Done in

vers libre, they are always
fading away, fainting, falling

but still gainfully employed
(though below minimum wage),

this choir invisible,
our heavenly hierarchy

of principalities and powers,
now the fairies of our fictions,

diminished and diminishing
(nixies, merfolk, pixies, naiads)

or pleasantly, devilishly bad
(brownie, goblin, imp, and sprite).

What a delight! What comfort,
this sacred parody, apotheosis.

In each other's bodies, we believe
there to be the limbs of angels,

sex a swift glistening of wet wings,
the spirit world suddenly coming

down to this: hot-pink kisses, seraphim
as Vargas girls, airbrushed, understanding.

Or, for the ladies, let them be done up
in white, lightly floating to the ceiling,

like Jordan Baker and that dangerous Daisy,
loosening into miracles of disappearance

from the despair of our daily lives
while we grind on, manufacturing meaning

in our celestial factories as housewives bake
trays of angels to hang on Christmas trees.

But I judge, and am myself judged,
when they are just our deep need for mystery,

only the blow-up dolls left over
from the explosion of our afterlife:

our better selves, our better lovers,
the replacements for our aging mothers,

all vaporized into angels,
vampirized into angel poems.

Well, so what if we are
making an easy mythology,

misusing spare parts of old creeds,
and our simple, contradictory spirits

in yarn-yellow wigs and plastic wings
are ham actors, last-minute stand-ins

for our exes, the winds, and destiny.
Let's play with our angels playfully,

for they cannot mean anything
more than we can possibly mean.

Self

The young man hasn't any.
It's out-of-date, outmoded, obsolete.
He's Consumer Culture, a roll of film

spilling out to the street, half man,
half machine, jacked in to a web
of circuitry, sound bites, advertising,

nada y nada, that old Hemingway
shotgun in the mouth, macho rock
of assertion, of groundbreaking.

Besides, this is good for me.
As a woman, I must appreciate
the loss of singular consciousness,

diminishment of issues, erasure
of personal narrative, the absurdity
of elegy (only bourgeois ego)

and all those phallocentric unities
old feminists and politicos cling to.
Far better, this suicide of sentiment,

the flat affect (yet how traditional
really, how Marlboro, how manly:
the blank face, dead screen).

Feminism's dead anyway.
I can say "bitch" with impunity.
Because who are you to say?

Who are you? It's all the same,
death and spaghetti, as we slide
from Hierarchy to Democracy.

Everything's nothing, and art
is anything. There's no gift,
artistry, reason for being,

only the post-Enlightenment
explosion of a color TV.
Look into a mirror and see:

> *a black cape*
> *the rhinoceros trembling*
> *an old can of paint*

(I could go on endlessly).
It's much better like this,
that's what you're telling me,

as it was for the women who stoked
forties' factories before going home
to slow suicides in the fifties,

who were free to please in the sixties,
not ask anything of seventies' men,
and in the eighties, able to be them.

Lover, let me ask you something.
When you come in me, do you
feel nothing? Is it white on white?

Nothing plunged into nothing?
What of this hard dark seed,
the ruby red pearl of love

I offer the construction of "you"?
Will you not swallow it?
Will you not love me?

When the World Lost Meaning

When the world lost meaning,
we were pretty much relieved.

God didn't fall from His place
as Our Father, Our Lord and King.

Not with a big bang at least.
He acquired immune deficiencies,

split from Mary, who receded (like a lady)
behind veils of her blue mystery,

let Jesus return to humanity, as He
felt Himself dissolving helplessly

into a Higher Being, then the Love
Between Us, ultimately a Cultural Heritage

passed down by mortal men and women
for male and female reasons.

You're bound to wonder many things.
Did the rings of Saturn stop turning?

Did the Northern Lights stop glittering?
Did Time and Space stop mattering?

No, although metaphors became similes,
and symbols dropped off their starry stands,

wobbling, fainthearted, undetermined,
uneasy in the gaseous atmosphere.

Death, of course, gasped a last *No*
and refused to transmute into anything.

No heaven, astral plane, second helpings.
Only collapse, rigor mortis, dissolution.

Sure, we thought of blowing out our brains,
maddened honeybees without a queen,

and some of us did. Others OD'd.
It was hard, yet it was easy,

for we'd been relieved of meaning
and no longer had to keep living,

finally free from karma, magic, harmony,
Catholic candles, devil worship, idolatry,

the power of positive thinking,
crystal imaging, New Age posturing,

poetic justice, fate, irony,
foresight, hindsight, insight

into the random, helpless, hapless times
that we always (didn't we? secretly?) feared

in our hard dark red hearts (broken
clocks, I say, deformed dwarf trees,

childhood's dime-store cinnamon candies)
really lacked all rhyme or reason.

So now we enjoy a pretty thing or two,
for pleasure always has been, still is, pleasing.

Lunatic Snow

first snowfall
packed snow
powder
drifting snow
snowdrift that blocks our way home
snowshoe snow
wind-snow, soft-moving, slow
snow that causes dogs to skid
golden snow
falling snow
fallen snow
rippled surface of snow
buried depth of snow
hart-hunting snow
the snow of loneliness
holy snowfall of the saints
the snow to restore virginity
red snow, or blood-rose
the snow of memory
succulent snow
serious snow
city snow
sleet
sheets of heart-divided snow
snow whose heart is hardening to ice
Russian snow
the snow of fairy tales
the snow of souls
snow that covers an opening
soft snow

very soft snow
snowflake (*)
glazed snow in a thaw
snow that wants to return to water
snow that longs for clouds
frost on the living
the snow we cannot comprehend
snow of the newly married
backsliding snow
snow that refuses to be known as snow
snow between toes
snow on clothes
light snow that is deep for walking
snow overhead and about to fall
avalanche
sex-snow, or lying down with angels
moon snow, a special kind
laughing snow
lunatic snow that steers you into questioning
snow that whispers the unknown names of snow

Providence

White lace curtains from Ann & Hope,
white-laced cars on Benefit Street,

a white nightgown pressed to my body.
Again, we find it is February.

Square wedding cake houses are cut
into pastels, begging to be boxed,

and would be if there were just
a God and She suckled a sweet tooth

for humanity's decaying architecture,
our most delicate of histories.

I'm afraid we are lost and alone.
I stand at the window half-frozen.

To my surprise, I find I am lying,
for this wintering world has awoken,

milky, wet, soft, adrift, and snowing
as you sleep, suddenly loved, in my bed.

My Summer as a Bride

Is this your first time?
She's actually asking this,
and asking this of me,
which is pretty surprising,

though I see what she's thinking,
I see what I'm doing. I'm trying
on wedding dresses, all traditional
in silhouette and sensibility.

It's a veritable garden
of crystal, gold, and pearl,
a designer's vocabulary of laces:
Venise, Alençon, Schiffli.

I am hooking myself
into a full-skirted ballerina,
scalloped sweetheart neckline,
hand-beaded and sequined.

Shining white satin rosettes
line the basque-waisted bodice,
and the multilayered, hand-sewn,
cathedral-length train of tulle

will be carried, as I gather,
by a whole fleet of fairies
for the queen: a tiara is even
propped atop my silly head.

Then a pale pink silk hat
with matching satin roses
takes its place as she laces me
into a shape-defining sheath,

pulling my resisting fingers
into gloves of hand-knit silken
mesh. Good heavens. Thousands
of worms have died for this.

The seas have been plumbed,
countless oyster beds plundered,
and weary women even more
wearied to create this creation,

to conspire in my transformation
into one of the white witches
beaming from the glossy photos
of bridal monthlies, the lucky

grooms tuxedoed shadows
at the edges of the pages.
There is no room for them.
They have no say in this.

The women stand alone,
lost in their contemplation
of *la pièce de résistance,*
a long-awaited coronation.

Or they may be celebrating
a private rite of initiation
into the secrets of wifery,
the patterning of a lady's days:

how to keep the silverware
gleaming, old husbands rolling
in money, lovers and children
both devoted quietly.

Either way, surely it's power,
it's victory. The women in white
are at the center of everything,
the universe itself offering up

its bounty to the bride, all
because a man, discreetly
receding to the margins
of a women's magazine,

has agreed to get married,
to take unto himself a wife,
a second self, a better half,
a helpmate, a bride.

Silk stockings are smoothing
up my thighs, roses sewing
themselves in my underthings
with gossamer-thin needles.

A fragrant bouquet is blooming
over my Venusian mound, now
maidenly shielded from the eyes
of all but the man I will marry.

Yes, it's my first time,
I answer breathlessly.
I can't help it. It's white magic.
I'm lost in my own reflection,

arms laden with ivory roses,
locks rolling themselves into gold
ringlets as if I were the princess
daughter of King Midas, white

diamonds of the first water drop
from my pearly lobes, and I am
smiling that smile of mystery,
past lovers fading away

into vague memories, then
impossibilities as my hymen
begins to gleam a silken honey,
that glistening web of virginity,

as I move forward toward
my husband-to-be, a man
who has decided to marry,
and, mysteriously, to marry me.

In Praise of My Young Husband

I know why all the old men want young girls,
why the other old men love young boys,
for I see how they are like the young girls,
having whispered into your ear, my dear,
and stroked your Chatterton pale chest,
the soft bowl of your Botticelli belly.

I know why men leave their old wives,
wives their old husbands, why women love
their men, why women love their women,
for you seem to me masculine, then again
feminine: your almond eyes, smooth cheeks.
I know why mothers do so love their sons,

and daughters their good fathers, and why
a bed is a good, good thing (as are
down pillows, quilts, clean sheets),
why heterosexuals believe they've found
a perfect symmetry of difference, why
homosexuals believe they have found

a perfect balance of mirroring, why
young lovers like to drink too much
and make a drunken, careless love,
why couples always cook so much,
and our lips dip in that slippery curve,
why the rest can seem like nothing more

than a morning lie we tell ourselves
so we will leave our beds and keep

an interest in our professional lives,
why many must make a dangerous love
and threaten these professional lives,
why all lovers will give it one more try,

why we are finally willing to fail,
why we will still let ourselves fall
in love, why I, surely old enough
(a cautious friend kindly implies)
to know better, can think of nothing
better than the buoyancy of your body,

the great gift of your gentleness, how
kind you are, in love with me, and why,
with a spinster's age and weight of sorrow,
in white below the green of your parents'
weeping willows, I will take these vows,
knowing nothing other than our love.

Dark Water

You hold me like a baby
in the lake. A bed of leaves

deepens our bodies into gold
as we circle in the dark water.

I lift one leg into the air,
and it pales to pink,

dip it below the surface,
and again there is the gold.

You are so light, you whisper
into the pearl of my pink ear,

and, believing I am weightless
at last, I lean my head

into the space all creation
seems to have made for it

above your left collarbone,
thankful to be afloat

in this new element,
near sunset, night's ink

etching out the dark green
of the trees, the sky itself

pale pink but darkening,
letting myself finally rest

within this ring, not afraid
of the black water snakes

who are known to be
equally fond of lingering.

When we leave this water,
I let you wrap my body

in the better towel and watch
as you bend down to loosen

a thistle from my pale pink foot,
my hand resting on your head,

which also has turned dark
gold in the early evening.

Then in our rented room,
you begin again, my body

darkening into gold
as I feel myself slipping

into this new element.
We are still newly married.

Deer

One of us claimed a moose.
The odd shape, the hugeness
made him know what he knew.

From the handyman came
a tale of the rabid raccoon
chattering its babble of anxiety.

Others chimed in with crazed coyotes,
then less rash talk of more ordinary
sightings: woodchucks, a possum.

Then the beautiful Bostonian
(whom I believed to be a lesbian
and admired for her choice

of an alternative lifestyle
and for her beauty,
sure she was struggling

to stop herself from falling
headlong in love with me
until I learned she too

had a husband
to whom she was
apparently happily married)

said she had seen
a porcupine. A porcupine!
The very word delighted.

We wanted her
to tell us how she knew
what she'd known.

It was the right size, she said,
but our hearts were hardened
to such belief. To our relief,

she added, *There were quills.*
Quills! A certainty!
Well, I could imagine

there were quills, she said,
then paused, probably
thinking of her husband

(to whom she was
apparently happily married)
as the rest of us

dissolved into silence
and deep discouragement
at this final ambiguity.

Would nothing ever be
clear and easy? So I,
who have seen nothing

(though I have believed
my heart pure enough
to deserve a sighting),

determine I will lie
and claim, *Oh, yeah,
last night, two or three*

of some kind of animal
when we meet again.
Of course, there's no need,

for in the morning, leaving
the bark-lined cabin where
Thornton Wilder apparently

just sat down and wrote
Our Town (a great American
classic and still good

for this little city,
I've often thought,
passing by Our Town Realty),

I step into nature,
scented with lemon
insect repellent, and let

myself believe there could be
four or five, half a dozen,
three or four fawns,

white-spotted babies,
a mama and a daddy,
gliding between the trees,

ladylike hooves silenced
with the sighing of the wind
through the leaves,

the whole family shivering
with joy and anticipation
of the moment when I will

close myself inside again,
knowing they are there
for me, they are waiting.

Dead Debutante

Blood sprayed down my yellow gown,
        which happens to look great on me
                though it's pinned in the back

and the nail polish has me lacquered in,
        I look thin, pale, hollow-eyed, when I arrive,
                pretty and scary, a faded girl

still waiting to come out in society.
        They are all his friends, but not really,
                fellow intellectuals

who've refused to wear anything too silly,
        only tokens of the evening:
                eye mask, funny hat, insect antennae.

They are smiling benignly
        and offering me a drink.
                I'm a poet. People expect of me

what's dramatic, overdone, and possibly
        damaging to my respectability,
                so everyone's generally friendly

except the woman who leaves
        each room that I walk in
                as though I truly am

the walking dead, a zombie deb.
    I think she thinks
        she's talking over my head.

Her hair is black and spiky.
    Her heels are black and spiky.
        She's leaning into him,

offering something to eat, drink,
    anything, everything, so I
        place my icy hand on his,

pearly lips in that simple, wifely grin:
    he's mine, I'm with him.
        Sweetly, he allows me

to encircle him.
    My dead wife, he says,
        and the party begins.

Vampires at the Beach

"Sunning" in Newport, we are the hesitant guests of friends who have
borne a child now at play in the waves, which makes everything all right

for them, there need be no embarrassment over a ridiculous attachment
to a small animal (delicate, purebred), none of the unease of difficult,

in-between relations. They are married, and that is that. White,
    heterosexual,
age-appropriate, professional, employed. Christ, they've bought a house.

Their boy, not yet three, is happy, dribbling watered sand into exquisite,
temporary mountains. The husband, father, dives into the sea, slowly
    receding,

while our inviting friend smoothes sunscreen over her body. She's careful,
and she's reasonable, asking us questions, lying back to catch a few rays

in the safely late day while we huddle in our clothes, black, long-sleeved.
As a concession to normalcy, we've slipped out of our shoes, rolled
    our socks

into balls and hidden them, our skin white as leprosy, our fine profiles
turned from the sun as our Pomeranian turns from a fan's gentle breeze.

We don't sun. We haven't brought our suits. I at least have an excuse:
skin disease, the stupidly incurable virus which comes and goes,
    leaving me

with a scattering of temporary red moles, so I keep my skin to myself,
     slathering
on special creams in the bright but otherwise painless light of my
     bathroom

before I ease my blessedly pale and relatively blemish-free body between
our conjugal sheets. For we too are married, white, straight, basically
     employed

(though he's still in school): the cultural elite one reads of in magazines.
We eat fresh basil, arugula, sun-dried tomatoes, and live in a pleasant,
     rented dinginess

—sunken sofa, broken crockery—along with our furry baby, thus
     driving
reproductive acquaintances to fury: he's a dog! a dog! we've given birth
     to nothing!

It's true, my husband doesn't want to, we don't know what we're
     doing,
we're immature, irresponsible, selfish. Look at us, squinting in our
     shades.

For all the locals know, we are happy heroin addicts (which we
     could be,
God knows, the love of sugar, our black clothes). An older man, pure
     mafioso,

helps his younger honey shake out of her sweats until she's dark and
    jiggly
in a silver swimsuit that shimmers like stars. I don't know where we are.

We've never been here before. No one is rude enough (though it is a
    rude state)
to ask us what the hell we think we're doing. They're content to lean
    back

in low beach chairs, limbs pink sausages, and stare. Are we sick?
    Abnormal?
Immoral? Bad influences? A blight to this beach? The thing is, I teach.

Sometimes I think I'm nearly everything a right-wing mama and
    papa fear
their daughter's English professor might be. Then again, with my
    shaved legs,

darkened eyes, red lipstick, my heterosexual coupling, basically
    drug-free
existence, insistence on academic competence, how could I be threatening?

My forehead's tightening, I'm burning, lost in thought, estranged,
    as usual,
from all that's around me. I don't know how to live in a godless universe

where everything is meaningless. *I don't believe in God,* I tell my helpless
therapist. *Are you a good person?* she asks, as if the question were pertinent,

as though she's been sleeping through my annihilation of faith and reason.
I'm not evil, is all I can come up with. Yes, it's painful, living like this,

it's not easy, but it's something: there are reasons to be afraid, reasons
to rage (you know how rigidly bitter we old battle-axes can be)

though there's still love, pleasure, good wine, wet sand, mixed feelings,
and the cold solace of knowing I'm on the right side of history.